MAP AND TRACK
RAIN FORESTS

HEATHER C. HUDAK
Crabtree Publishing Company
www.crabtreebooks.com

CRABTREE
PUBLISHING COMPANY
WWW.CRABTREEBOOKS.COM

Author: Heather C. Hudak

Editors: Sarah Eason, Honor Head, Melissa Boyce

Proofreader and indexer: Wendy Scavuzzo

Editorial director: Kathy Middleton

Design: Jessica Moon

Cover design: Katherine Berti

Photo research: Jean Coppendale

Prepress and print coordination: Katherine Berti

Written, developed, and produced by Calcium

Every attempt was made to verify the accuracy of
the maps from multiple sources. Sources may differ.

Photo Credits:

b=Bottom, l=Left, r=Right, m=Middle, t=Top

Inside: U. S. Fish and Wildlife Service: Tom MacKenzie: p. 11t; Shutterstock: p. 14, 26b; Matt Amery: p. 24; Australian Camera: p. 4; Bildagentur Zoonar GmbH: p. 18t; bteimages: p. 10t; Handoko Ramawidjaya Bumi: p. 20b; Pipat Chanpong: p. 10b; Jo Crebbin: p. 1b, 9t, 29; Sebastian Delgado C: p. 7; djavitch: p. 22b; Efimovba Anna: p. 15t; Frontpage: p. 28b; Ken Griffiths: p. 18b; Laranik: p. 12; Marktucan: p. 5t; MarclSchauer: p. 17t; Milosz Maslanka: pp. 1r, 15b; MattiaATH: p. 19b; Alexander Mazurkevich: pp. 3, 20t; Morlaya: p. 22t; Myimages-Micha: p. 9b; NaturesMomentsuk: p. 23; Onyx9: pp. 1l, 17b; PhilipYb Studio: p. 28t; PhotocechCZ: p. 13b; Poeticpenguin: p. 25t; Salparadis: p. 5b; Jeff Schultes: p. 13tl; TLWilson Photography: p. 26t; Sergey Uryadnikov: p. 16; Juan Vilata: p. 25b; Michail Vorobyev: p. 21; Dennis van de Water: p. 11b; Vladimir Wrangel: p. 8; Milan Zygmunt: p. 27; Wikimedia Commons: JJ Harrison (jjharrison89@facebook.com): p. 19t

Maps: Jessica Moon, Katherine Berti

Cover: Shutterstock

Library and Archives Canada Cataloguing in Publication

Hudak, Heather C., 1975-, author
    Map and track rain forests / Heather C. Hudak.

(Map and track biomes and animals)
Includes index.
Issued in print and electronic formats.
ISBN 978-0-7787-5370-4 (hardcover).--
ISBN 978-0-7787-5382-7 (softcover).--
ISBN 978-1-4271-2204-9 (HTML)

    1. Rain forest ecology--Juvenile literature. 2. Rain forest animals--Juvenile literature. 3. Rain forests--Maps--Juvenile literature. 4. Cartography--Juvenile literature. I. Title.

QH541.5.R27H83 2019   j577.34   C2018-905638-X
                                              C2018-905639-8

Library of Congress Cataloging-in-Publication Data

Names: Hudak, Heather C., 1975- author.
Title: Map and track rain forests / Heather C. Hudak.
Description: New York : Crabtree Publishing Company, 2019. |
    Series: Map and track biomes and animals | Includes index.
Identifiers: LCCN 2018049862 (print) | LCCN 2018051962 (ebook) |
    ISBN 9781427122049 (Electronic) |
    ISBN 9780778753704 (hardcover) |
    ISBN 9780778753827 (pbk.)
Subjects: LCSH: Rain forests--Juvenile literature. |
    Rain forest ecology--Juvenile literature.
Classification: LCC QH86 (ebook) | LCC QH86 .H84 2019 (print) |
    DDC 577.34--dc23
LC record available at https://lccn.loc.gov/2018049862

Crabtree Publishing Company
www.crabtreebooks.com   1-800-387-7650

Printed in the U.S.A./032019/CG20190118

Published in Canada
Crabtree Publishing
616 Welland Ave.
St. Catharines, Ontario
L2M 5V6

Published in the United States
Crabtree Publishing
PMB 59051
350 Fifth Avenue, 59th Floor
New York, New York 10118

Published in the United Kingdom
Crabtree Publishing
Maritime House
Basin Road North, Hove
BN41 1WR

Published in Australia
Crabtree Publishing
Unit 3–5 Currumbin Court
Capalaba
QLD 4157

Contents

What are Rain Forests?

Think of an ocean covered in ice, snowy forests, treeless **grasslands**, and a **parched** desert where it hardly ever rains. These regions are different from each other, but they have one thing in common—they are all **biomes**.

Amazing Biomes

A biome is an area that can be **classified** based on the types of plants and animals that live there. The **climate**, soil type, and the amount of available water determine what plants and animals live in the area. A rain forest is a biome where thick forests of tall trees cover the land, and there is a lot of rain all year round. Rain forests have a wide variety of plant life that provides food and shelter for millions of different animals.

Bursting with Life

From beetles to bears, rain forests are home to as many as 30 million plant, animal, and bird **species**. Some, such as tree boas, are most active during the day. This helps them avoid birds of **prey** and other animals that hunt at night. About 80 percent of the world's insect species live in rain forests, too. Each species has **adapted** to living in a rain forest. Walking sticks are insects that look like tree branches. Glasswing butterflies have see-through wings, so they are hard to spot against trees and flowers.

In the Trees

Many different animals live in the trees. Sloths move through the forest slowly, using their long claws to grasp tree branches. They are covered in green **algae**, so **predators** cannot spot them.

Rain forests are home to about 50 percent of all animal species found on Earth.

4

RAINFOREST ANIMALS

The world's rain forests are home to a huge variety of animals, from enormous alligators to tiny insects. In this book, you will learn about many of these rainforest animals. The "Map and Track" features will show you where rainforest animals live. Build up your map-reading skills as you track their movements across the biome.

Jaguars are found mainly in the Amazon rain forest.

Poison dart frogs live in tropical rain forests. They are one of many species at risk because rain forests are being destroyed.

MORE RAINFOREST ANIMALS

As we travel around the world's rain forests, you will get a chance to take a close-up look at some of the **endangered** or threatened animals that live there in the "Stop and Spot" features throughout the book.

Rain Forests of the World

There are two main types of rain forests—**temperate** and **tropical**. Tropical rain forests are hot, **humid**, and wet all year round. There is not much difference in temperature from day to night. Temperate rain forests have a cooler climate with four seasons. Summers are short, hot, and foggy. Winters are long and wet.

Where in the World?

Tropical rain forests are found mainly near the **equator**. South and Central America, Africa, Asia, and Australia are home to many tropical rain forests. Temperate rain forests are found in coastal areas, such as the Pacific Northwest, from northern California to Canada and Alaska.

Plenty of Plants

Hundreds of different types of trees live in tropical rain forests. They are best known for their tall **evergreen** trees and flowering plants, such as orchids. Temperate rain forests have only 10 to 20 different types of trees. **Conifer** trees are common, along with plants such as mosses and ferns. Temperate rain forests also have **deciduous** and evergreen trees.

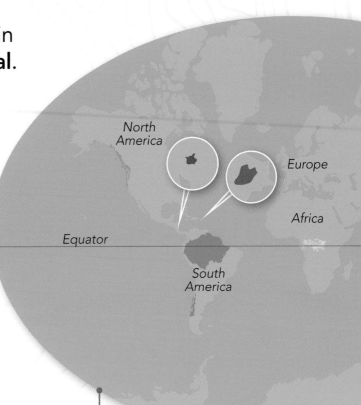

North America

Europe

Africa

Equator

South America

Antarctica

This map shows all the rain forests we will explore in this book.

Key
Tropical rain forests:
Amazon Rain Forest
El Yunque National Forest
Monteverde Cloud Forest
   Reserve
Sinharaja Rain Forest
Congo Rain Forest
Daintree Rain Forest
Harapan Rain Forest
Temperate rain forests:
Pacific Coastal Temperate
   Rain Forest
Valdivian Rain Forest
Primorsky Krai

6

Asia

Australia/
Oceania

Spider monkeys use their long limbs and tails to climb the tall trees. Their tails are specially adapted to grab onto branches.

Tree Dwellers

Plants grow in layers in rain forests. Trees grow from 60 to 150 feet (18 to 46 m) tall. Most tropical rainforest animals live in the **canopy**, which is at the very top of the trees. There is a lot of sunshine and rain in the canopy throughout the year. Animals can find plenty of fruit and nuts to eat in this part of the rain forest. Some animals, such as spider monkeys, spend all their time in the canopy. They use their long tails to hang from the trees. Toco toucans also live high in the canopy. They use their large, curved beaks to reach fruit that birds with smaller beaks cannot reach.

Forest Floor Feast

In temperate rain forests, most animals live on the forest floor. There, the tall trees protect them from wind and rain. Many birds and small **mammals**, such as squirrels and chipmunks, feed on the seeds that fall to the ground from the plants and trees. Slugs are a yellow, brown, or green color to help them blend in with leaves and earth on the forest floor. The humidity keeps slugs from drying out.

Amazon Rain Forest

The Amazon rain forest is a tropical rain forest that stretches across South America. It is the largest rain forest in the world. No other place on Earth has more plant and animal life. However, human activities are threatening many of these species.

Water World

The Amazon rain forest has the largest number of **freshwater** fish in the world. This is because the Amazon River basin flows through the Amazon rain forest. The Amazon River basin is an area that drains into the Amazon River, which is one of the largest and longest rivers in the world. The basin also has more than 1,100 rivers and streams.

Fish Life

Many Amazon fish have adapted to a diet of fruits and seeds that fall from low-hanging trees along the riverbanks. The fruit and seeds float on top of the water and are easy for fish to eat. Piranhas are found in the Amazon River. They have a very good sense of smell. This helps them find food even in murky water. Piranhas hunt in groups, so that they can attack larger animals, such as cattle, that drink at the water's edge.

Scary Snakes

Lizards, caimans, turtles, and snakes are common throughout the Amazon rain forest. Green anacondas are snakes that live in **swamps** and streams. They are good swimmers. They breathe through openings in the top of their heads while hiding underwater, watching for animals on the land. They feed on deer, wild pigs, and jaguars.

The anaconda is the largest snake in the world. It can grow to more than 29 feet (9 m) long.

BALD UAKARIS

Bald uakaris are small monkeys found in the rain forest near rivers, ponds, and lakes. Veins under their skin give their faces a bright red color. The healthiest uakaris have the reddest faces, so they are more likely to attract a **mate**. Uakaris have shorter tails than most monkeys, so they use their strong arms and legs to move quickly and easily through the trees instead. Their jaws are so strong, they can crack open a Brazil nut.

Bald uakaris only come down to the ground to find food.

Shrinking Forest

More than half of the Amazon rain forest has been destroyed since the 1950s. **Global warming**, **mining**, **logging**, and farming are the main activities destroying the forest. As much as 65 percent of the area is at risk of turning into treeless land in the next 50 years. Many countries are working together to try to save the rain forest. Giant otters, South American tapirs, and pygmy sloths are some of the animals at risk of **habitat** loss and possible **extinction**.

South American tapirs live near water where they can eat, bathe, and rest.

El Yunque National Forest

The El Yunque Mountains in northeast Puerto Rico are home to a small but important tropical rain forest. Eight rivers run through the forest, and they provide 20 percent of Puerto Rico's water. The rain forest's landscape includes waterfalls, **ravines**, and canyons.

*Coqui are very well **camouflaged** against forest tree trunks.*

Small and Mighty

Many rainforest animals perch on tree branches or hide under leaves. One of the smallest forest animals in El Yunque is the coqui tree frog. It is only 1 to 2 inches (2.5 to 5 cm) long and weighs just 2 to 4 ounces (56 to 113 g). These tiny frogs are famous for their big voices. They begin to sing when the Sun goes down each night and do not stop until the next morning. It is not known why they sing. Coqui can change colors to blend in with their surroundings. They also have special pads on their feet that stick to trees and wet leaves to help them climb better.

Slow and Steady

El Yunque is home to large tree snails. Their shells can measure up to 4 inches (10 cm) in diameter. They move around on a special foot that makes slime to help the snail slide more easily from place to place. Tree snails use their rough tongues to scrape leaves, algae, and flowers off the trees.

Tree snails can live for as long as 10 years in the moist rain forest.

PUERTO RICAN PARROTS

There were about 1 million Puerto Rican parrots living in Puerto Rico and nearby islands at the start of the 1500s. There were many forests with fruits and seeds for the birds to eat, and large, old trees with holes where the birds would nest. Now, because of **deforestation** and natural disasters, there are only about 30 Puerto Rican parrots left in El Yunque. Scientists are raising the birds in **captivity** and releasing them into the wild to increase numbers.

The Puerto Rican parrot is one of the most endangered bird species in the world.

From its mountain peaks to the low canyons, El Yunque National Forest is home to a huge variety of different animals.

Night Lights

At night, parts of El Yunque are lit by thousands of large, glowing beetles called cucubanos, a species of click beetle. These long, skinny insects have two glowing dots near the upper part of their body. The light from the glowing dots can be used to scare away predators. Cucubanos can make their light brighter when they feel they are in danger. They come out during the rainy season, from April through June, and lay their eggs in the soil. Their eggs and **larvae** also glow.

Monteverde Cloud Forest Reserve

At the tropical Monteverde Cloud Forest Reserve in Costa Rica, tourists can take a walk in the clouds. In the reserve, clouds gather in the canopy of trees. They drip onto the plants and ground below.

Rare Forests

Cloud forests are found high up where warm winds blow against mountains. This causes the air to rise and change into moisture to form clouds. Cloud forests are cooler than other rain forests, and this helps form mist and fog. They are still very humid. Cloud forests usually have fast, clear, shallow rivers that add more moisture to the air.

Orchid Home

In the Monteverde Cloud Forest Reserve, thick clouds keep most of the sunlight from reaching the ground, so it is very damp all the time. These conditions are just right for epiphytes to grow. Epiphytes are plants that grow on top of other plants. They get their **nutrients** from the air, rain, and rainforest **mulch**. Lichens and orchids are epiphytes.

Wild Cats

Monteverde is home to six species of the cat family: ocelots, jaguars, oncillas, margays, pumas, and jaguarundis. The forest gives them cover for hunting and plenty of prey to hunt, such as monkeys, birds, and tapirs. The margay has flexible ankle joints that allow its feet to turn backward so it can move through the treetops as easily as a squirrel. Ocelots live on or near the ground. They have a spotted gray coat with black rings and beige patches that help them blend in with their surroundings.

Orchids are beautiful flowers that thrive in the moist conditions of the rain forest.

QUETZALS

MAP AND TRACK

This map shows the protected sites of the quetzal in Costa Rica.

The quetzal lives in the canopy of evergreen forests throughout the Americas. However, it likes the tall, old trees of the cloud rain forest best. The dead trees have soft wood that the quetzal needs to build its nest. Its beak and claws are not strong enough to dig into live trees. Humans are clearing away the forest for farming and timber, and this is destroying the trees the quetzal needs.

Caribbean Sea

Monteverde Cloud Forest Reserve

Costa Rica

Pacific Ocean

Key
Protected sites

The quetzal uses soft dead wood to build nests.

Ocelots have excellent hearing and can see well in the dark, which helps them find prey at night.

Sinharaja Rain Forest

At one time, rain forests covered much of Sri Lanka's land. Over time, humans began to cut down the trees for timber. They cleared the forests for farming and other activities. Today, the Sinharaja rain forest is the last large tropical rain forest in the country. Located in the southwest corner of Sri Lanka, the rain forest has a wide variety of plant and animal life.

Ears and Trunks

Indian elephants are well adapted to life in the rain forest. With their huge ears, the elephants can hear even the softest sounds, so they can tell if predators such as tigers are nearby. Elephants flap their ears to cool their blood and get it flowing throughout their bodies. They use their long, thick trunks to find food that is hard to reach, high in the trees and low on the ground. They also use their trunks to talk to other elephants and warn them of threats. Indian elephants are endangered due to habitat loss. Many elephants are hunted for their valuable ivory tusks.

Alarm Call

Agamid lizards have strong legs and tails for climbing trees. The endangered whistling lizard is one of about 350 lizard species that are part of the agamid family. The lizard gets its name from the high-pitched whistling sound it makes when it is angry or threatened. Whistling lizards are tree-dwelling **reptiles** that live mainly in wet, shaded forest areas. They feed mostly on birds and insects. They are endangered due to habitat loss.

Orange-billed babblers are noisy birds. They constantly chirp, chatter, and squeak!

14

WESTERN PURPLE-FACED LANGURS

Western purple-faced langurs are a type of monkey. They eat leaves that can be hard to **digest**, so they have a special stomach that helps break down plant material. Sometimes, they eat soil from **termite mounds** that contains **minerals** that help them digest leaves. More than 90 percent of their habitat has been lost to deforestation. As a result, many purple-faced langurs have been forced to live near humans in yards and on rooftops.

The endangered purple-faced langurs live only in the tropical forests of Sri Lanka.

Birds Flock Together

Orange-billed babblers and crested drongoes often work together to find food. In the morning, drongoes call out to wake up the other birds in the flock. They also send out an alarm call if they spot a predator. The other birds freeze, so they will not be spotted. They wait until the drongo gives an all-clear sound before moving on. The noise and movement of the large flock forces many insects into the open where they can be snatched up.

The trees of the Sinharaja rain forest canopy grow as tall as 148 feet (45 m).

Congo Rain Forest

The tropical Congo rain forest is the second-largest rain forest in the world. It stretches across six countries in Central Africa but is mainly in the north of the Democratic Republic of the Congo (DRC).

High and Low
The Congo rain forest has mountains, **lowlands**, and the mighty Congo River running through it. It is home to the greatest number of **primates**, birds, fish, and swallowtail butterflies in all of Africa.

Bonobos are one of the primates that live in the Congo rain forest.

BONOBOS

This map shows where bonobos live in Africa.

Bonobos are similar to chimpanzees but are smaller, darker, and have longer limbs. Bonobos are the animals most closely **related** to humans. Bonobos live only in the forests south of the Congo River. They are endangered due to **poaching** and deforestation. There are only 15,000 to 20,000 bonobos in the Congo rain forest today.

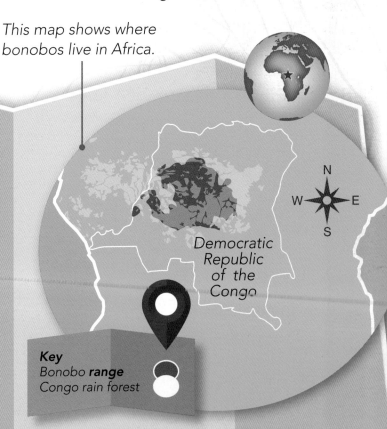

Democratic Republic of the Congo

Key
Bonobo **range**
Congo rain forest

Grasping Tongues

Okapis live only in the rain forest of the Democratic Republic of the Congo. They look like a cross between a giraffe and a zebra. Their tongues are able to grasp objects. This is useful for stripping the leaves, stems, and buds from trees and plants. There were about 45,000 okapis when they were first discovered in 1900. Today, there are only about 10,000 left due to habitat loss and a high risk of disease.

Okapis are the only living relative of the giraffe.

Great Gorillas

The Congo rain forest is the only place in the world where all three types of gorillas can be found. They are the mountain gorillas, western lowland gorillas, and eastern lowland gorillas. Mountain gorillas live high in the mountains. They have a lot of thick fur to help them survive the freezing temperatures. Western lowland gorillas live in the thickest and most **remote** parts of the Congo rain forest. This makes them hard to find and study. Eastern lowland gorillas have thin hair that helps keep them cool in warmer temperatures. Over the past 50 years, the range of all these gorilla species has decreased to a tiny amount of their original size because of **illegal** logging, poaching, and wars.

Gorillas, such as this mountain gorilla, have excellent eyesight, which is useful for finding food in the rain forest.

Daintree Rain Forest

The tropical Daintree rain forest in Queensland, Australia, has the largest number of rare and nearly extinct plants and animals in the world. Some species have lived there for millions of years, such as the idiot fruit. Fossils show that this plant was around when dinosaurs roamed Earth.

Sliding Dragons

Lizards named Boyd's forest dragons tuck in their legs and slowly slide to the other side of the tree when they feel threatened. Unlike many other lizards, they do not lie in sunlight to warm up. Instead, their bodies adapt to whatever the air temperature is. This is because it is not always easy to find sunlight through the thick forest cover.

Boyd's forest dragons look so much like tree trunks, they can be hard to spot in the rain forest.

Scary Lizard

One of the scariest-looking reptiles in the Daintree is the frilled lizard. When threatened, this lizard opens the frill around its neck to make its head look much larger. However, it is not dangerous at all. As soon as it feels safe, it runs away on its hind legs. Frilled lizards have only a few predators due to their large size. These include large snakes, dingoes, foxes, and birds of prey.

Frilled lizards can change color to blend in with their environment, so it is hard for predators to spot them.

Quolls

The cat-sized spotted-tailed quoll is the largest **carnivorous marsupial** in Australia. Quolls spend most of their time on the forest floor. However, they have ridges on their long, pink footpads that help them climb high into the canopy to hunt possums.

Spotted-tailed quolls hunt mainly at night.

CASSOWARIES

The cassowary is a large, flightless bird. As tourism has increased in the Daintree rain forest, the cassowary's habitat has become smaller. Land is being used for roads and hotels. Cars, buses, and ferries are **polluting** the water. The cassowary eats more than 100 species of plants. The seeds of these plants are then scattered through their **dung**. The seeds grow into plants that provide food and shelter for rain forest animals. This makes the cassowary a **keystone species**.

N
W——E
S

Daintree rain forest

Australia

Key
Cassowary range

This map shows the cassowary range in Australia.

The cassowary is about 6.6 feet (2 m) tall. Only about 4,000 of these birds remain in the wild today.

Harapan Rain Forest

At one time, Sumatra, in Indonesia, was covered with rain forests. Trees have been cut down to make way for farms and buildings, so now only a small amount of the tropical Harapan rain forest is left.

Rotting Corpse

The Harapan has more than 600 tree species. Loggers have cut down many of the big, old trees that create the dark, moist environment the plants that grow there need. As a result, many plants have started to disappear. One of these is the endangered **corpse** flower, which smells like a rotting corpse. The smell attracts insects to the plant so they can carry its **pollen** to other flowers.

Tusk Tasks

The Sumatran elephant is the smallest of the Asian elephants. The elephants are suffering from loss of habitat, and many are being poached for their tusks, which are very valuable. They use their tusks to strip wood from trees to eat. They also use them to dig into the ground to find water in the dry season.

Last of the Rhinos

The Sumatran rhinoceros is the smallest and hairiest of the rhino species. It is also the most threatened, with fewer than 100 left in the wild. Their habitat is being cut down for farmland and homes, and they are illegally killed for their horns.

The rhino's horns are valuable in Asian medicine.

The corpse flower is the largest flower in the world. It can be more than 3 feet (1 m) across and can weigh as much as 22 pounds (10 kg).

MALAYAN SUN BEARS

MAP AND TRACK

Malayan sun bears are the smallest bears in the world. They get their name from the light-colored patch of fur on their chest that is said to look like the rising Sun. Sun bears have long claws for tearing apart trees and termite nests to find food. They use their long tongues to lick honey from beehives or termites from their nests. There are only about 550 bears still living in the rain forest.

N W E S

Harapan rain forest

Sumatra

Indian Ocean

The Malayan sun bear's range in Sumatra has decreased due to logging and farming.

Key
Original range
Today's range

Malayan sun bears are about half the size of the American black bear. They use their long, sharp claws to climb trees in search of food.

Pacific Coastal Temperate Rain Forest

This rain forest stretches along the coast of the Pacific Ocean from Alaska, through British Columbia, Canada, to northern California. It is the largest coastal temperate rain forest on Earth. Most of the trees there are conifers because of its cold and snowy winter climate.

Made for Snow

Conifers are cone-shaped, and their branches bend easily. This helps to keep snow from piling up on the tree and breaking it. Conifers also have thick bark to protect them from the cold.

Plentiful Fish

Salmon hatch in the rain forest's freshwater streams. They then make their way to the ocean, where they spend most of their lives. They return to the rain forest's fresh waters to **spawn** and die. The rotting bodies act as nutrients for rainforest plants—80 percent of the **nitrogen** forests need to grow comes from salmon. The Pacific coastal temperate rain forest has one of the largest grizzly bear populations due to its salmon supply that is food for the bears.

Conifer needles have a waxy coating that stops water loss when the weather is cold.

*Grizzly bears wade into rivers to catch salmon. The fish help the bears build the fat they need to survive while they **hibernate** through winter.*

SPIRIT BEARS

MAP AND TRACK

The rare spirit bear is also a big fan of salmon. This American black bear has a special **gene** that makes its fur white. The bear's light color may help it catch more fish because it blends in better with the water than bears with black or brown coats. The spirit bear has two other names: the Kermode bear, or the Tsimshian Coastal First Nations word *moskgm'ol*, which means "white bear."

N W E S

Canada

Pacific coastal temperate rain forest

United States of America

Threats to the spirit bear include loss of habitat due to logging activity.

Key
Spirit bear range
Spirit bear sightings

Experts believe there are fewer than 400 spirit bears in the wild.

Valdivian Rain Forest

The Valdivian rain forest is the only temperate rain forest in South America. It stretches through parts of Chile and Argentina, with the Pacific Ocean on one side and the Andean Mountains on the other side. This rain forest has bamboo trees, snow-capped volcanoes, and icy **glaciers**.

Drilling for Food

Magellanic woodpeckers are the largest woodpeckers in South America and one of the largest in the world. They mainly feed on insect larvae that live inside tree trunks. Their bills act like a chisel to drill into the wood to get to the larvae. Once the woodpecker has made a hole, it uses its sticky tongue to pull the larvae out of the tree trunk. Its tongue is four times longer than its bill, so it can reach deep inside the tree.

The Magellanic woodpecker has thick feathers covering its nostrils to keep wood chips from getting inside.

Mistletoe Marsupial

The monito del monte (Spanish for "little mountain monkey") is a mouselike marsupial that lives only in southern South America. They eat the seeds of most fruit. The seeds pass through their bodies undamaged and are spread through their dung. This is especially important for the mistletoe plant in the forests of Chile and Argentina. There, monitos del monte are the only animals that spread the plant's seeds. More than 100 types of animals need the mistletoe for food and shelter, making the monito del monte a keystone species.

SOUTHERN PUDUS

Southern pudus are so small they often stand on their hind legs or jump onto fallen trees to reach for food. Their low, round bodies let them move easily through the rainforest undergrowth. Southern pudus are found only in the Valdivian temperate rain forest. Their diet includes bark, twigs, buds, blossoms, and fruit. The southern pudu is threatened, mainly due to its shrinking habitat.

The southern pudu is the smallest deer species. It is just 14 to 18 inches (36 to 46 cm) tall.

*Today, only about 40 percent of the Valdivian temperate rain forest remains. Logging is a major threat. **Conservation** groups are working together to help protect the area.*

Primorsky Krai

About 80 percent of Primorsky Krai, in Siberia, is covered in temperate forest. Most of Primorsky Krai's forest is classified as rain forest. The temperature there is usually between 34 ° and 41 °Fahrenheit (1 ° and 5 °C) all year round. It has more than 500 natural features, such as volcanoes, lakes, rivers, caves, and waterfalls.

Living Together

The forests of Primorsky Krai are the only places on Earth where leopards, brown bears, and tigers live in the same region. Amur leopards are the most endangered big cats in the world. There are only 25 to 40 left in the wild. They have longer legs than other leopards for walking in the snow. Their coat changes color with the seasons to help them blend in with their surroundings.

Keeping Warm

Amur leopards prey mainly on roe deer. However, they will eat other animals if they are hungry enough, including wild boars, musk deer, Sitka deer, and goatlike animals called gorals. Roe deer have a coat made up of hollow hairs that help protect them from the cold.

The Amur leopard's coloring helps it hide against its surroundings (top) as it hunts prey, such as roe deer (bottom).

SIBERIAN TIGERS

About 80 percent of the world's last Siberian tigers are found in the forests of Primorsky Krai. Over the past 100 years, their population has declined by more than 95 percent. Today, only 480 to 540 Siberian tigers remain in the wild. Deforestation and poaching are major threats to these tigers. The Russian government has started programs to stop the hunting of these endangered animals, and to stop the logging of their habitat.

Russia

China

Primorsky Krai

North Korea

South Korea

N W E S

The range of the Siberian tiger has decreased since the 1800s.

Key
1800s range
Current range

Different Trees

Despite the freezing-cold conditions, at least 2,500 different types of plants grow in Primorsky Krai. **Broad-leaved** trees are most common at lower levels where there is warm, wet weather in summer. These trees have wide, green leaves to take in as much sunlight as they can during the growing season. As the weather cools, broad-leaved trees lose their leaves. In winter, the trees go into a **dormant** state to save energy. Conifers grow at the higher, colder levels.

Siberian tigers have thick fur and a layer of fat to help them keep warm in the cold.

Rain Forests in Danger

Millions of plants and animals need rain forests to survive. However, fires, logging, farming, mining, and other human activities mean that rain forests around the world are shrinking. This is a constant threat to rainforest wildlife.

Save Our Rain Forests

Conservation groups work with local people and governments to protect plants and animals in rain forests. They set up wildlife reserves where animals cannot be hunted. They plant new trees in areas that have been cut down. They help create laws to save land from logging and other activities.

Disappearing Forests

Some rain forests date back tens of millions of years. Yet, they could disappear in the next 30 to 50 years. In the Congo rain forest alone, as much as 50 percent of the land has been set aside for logging. In the Amazon rain forest, cattle graze on 80 percent of the deforested land, and their **waste** pollutes local rivers.

Global Warming

Earth's temperature is getting warmer. This means rain forest trees and flowers are **blooming** earlier or later than ever before. This is a big problem for animals that need fruit, **nectar**, and seeds to survive. Some animals are still hibernating when the plants bloom, causing them to miss their chance to feed. Other animals have not yet been born or hatched and so cannot find food when they need it.

Around the world, deforestation causes about 40 species to disappear each day (top). This is often done to make way for cattle farms (bottom).

Now it is your turn. You can create a map to track endangered rain forest animals. Here is what you need to do:

1. Choose one of the rain forests in this book.

2. Create a map to show the rain forest (see page 6 for help).

3. Research the animals that live in the rain forest you have chosen. Which ones are endangered? Choose two or three endangered animals to track.

4. Color in the map to show where they are found. See the box below for links to maps for your chosen animals.

5. Make a key to show what the different colors mean.

If you chose to track the hyacinth macaw, your map would look like this.

Guyana
Venezuela
Suriname
Colombia
French Guiana
Ecuador
N
W E
S
Brazil
Peru
Bolivia
Paraguay

Key
Amazon rain forest
Macaw range

THE IUCN

The International Union for Conservation of Nature (IUCN) is a great source of information for your map. The IUCN is an international group of scientists that track animals and decide whether they are endangered. They produce reports on many different species, including maps to show where they currently live. The website for their "Red List," where you can search by species, is on page 31.

Glossary

Please note: Some **boldfaced** words are defined where they appear in the text.

adapted Changed over time to better suit an environment

algae Simple plants without roots or stems

biomes Large geographical areas with the same general landscape, climate, and life

blooming Growing leaves and flowers

broad-leaved Having wide, broad leaves

camouflaged Blended in with the natural environment

canopy The highest layer of branches in a forest or on a tree

captivity Held in place and not free to leave

carnivorous Eating other animals

classified Arranged in a certain order

climate The usual weather conditions in a region

conifer Plants that bear cones and have needlelike or scalelike leaves

conservation Protecting nature and wildlife

corpse A dead body

deciduous Plants with broad leaves that drop in the fall and grow back in spring

deforestation Clearing trees from a forest

digest Break down food that has been eaten into substances the body can use

dormant An inactive or sleeplike state

dung Animal droppings or waste

endangered In danger of dying out

equator An imaginary line around the middle of Earth

evergreen Plants that have green leaves all year round

extinction When no living members are left on Earth

freshwater From a body of water with no salt

gene A part of every person that carries the features of a living thing

glaciers Large, slow-moving bodies of ice

global warming Earth's temperature increasing due to gases trapped in the air

grasslands Land with mainly grass and very few trees

habitat The natural environment of an animal or plant

hibernate Spend the winter in a sleeplike or inactive state

humid Lots of moisture in the air

illegal Against the law

keystone species An animal or plant that other animals and plants cannot survive without

larvae Young insects that look very different from their adult forms

logging Cutting down trees for timber

lowlands Flat land no higher than sea level

mammals Warm-blooded animals that feed their young with milk and have hair or fur

marsupial A mammal that has a pouch to carry its young

mate A partner to breed with

minerals Solid substances found in nature that are neither a plant or animal

mining Digging for coal and minerals

mulch Rotting materials on the forest floor

nectar Sweet fluid found in plants

nitrogen A chemical that makes up Earth's atmosphere and is found in all living things

nutrients Substances that living things need to grow and survive

parched Dry; having very little water

poaching Hunting illegally

pollen Fine dust from plants

polluting Making dirty and harmful

predators Animals that kill and eat other animals

prey Animals that are hunted and killed by other animals for food

primates Groups of mammal species that include monkeys, apes, and humans

range An area where an animal travels

ravines Small, deep, steep-sided valleys

related Belonging to the same family

remote Far away from others

reptiles Cold-blooded animals that have a dry scaly skin, such as tortoises, snakes, and lizards

reserve Land set aside to keep animals safe

spawn To lay eggs

species A distinct type of living thing

swamps Land that is always wet and often partly covered with water

termite mounds Homes made by termites

waste Food material eliminated from the body after being eaten and processed

Learning More

Books

Bailey, Gerry. *Tangled in the Rainforest: Can science save your life?* (Science to the Rescue). Crabtree Publishing Company, 2014.

Calver, Paul, and Toby Reynolds. *Rainforests* (Visual Explorers). Barron's Educational Series, 2015.

Hyde, Natalie. *Amazon Rainforest Research Journal* (Ecosystems Research Journal). Crabtree Publishing Company, 2017.

Spilsbury, Louise, and Richard Spilsbury. *Forest Biomes* (Earth's Natural Biomes). Crabtree Publishing Company, 2018.

Websites

www.coolkidfacts.com/rainforest-facts-for-kids
Discover amazing facts about rain forests and the animals that live there.

www.iucnredlist.org
Explore the IUCN's Red List of animals that are threatened, endangered, or nearly extinct.

wwf.panda.org/our_work/forests/importance_forests/tropical_rainforest
Investigate tropical rain forests and why they need to be protected.

www.rainforest-alliance.org/kids
Learn more about rain forests with games, activities, and virtual visits.

Index

ABOUT THE AUTHOR

Heather C. Hudak has written hundreds of books for children and edited thousands more. When she is not writing, she enjoys traveling all over the world. Heather has been to more than 50 countries. She has roamed the African savanna in Kenya, hiked the Rocky Mountains in Canada, sailed across the Atlantic Ocean, and explored the rain forests of Costa Rica.